AF428396

Adam Smith and His Theory of the Free Market

Social Studies for Kids

Children's Philosophy Books

Speedy Publishing LLC

40 E. Main St. #1156

Newark, DE 19711

www.speedypublishing.com

Copyright 2017

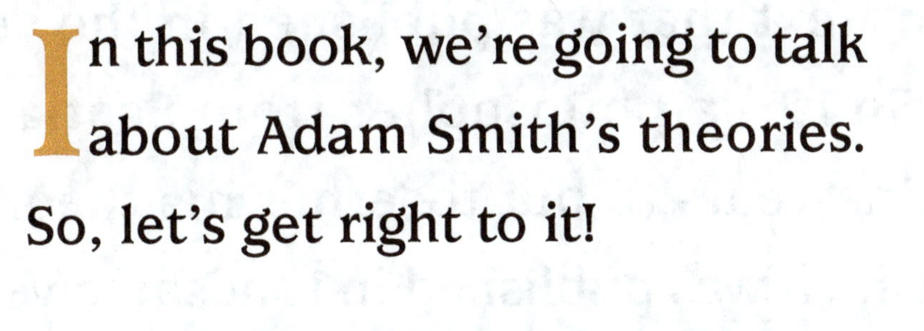
In this book, we're going to talk about Adam Smith's theories.
So, let's get right to it!

The Declaration of Independence wasn't the only important text that was published in the year 1776. Adam Smith, a philosopher from Scotland, worked for nine years to put together his theories into a book, which was published in that same year.

THE DECLARATION OF INDEPENDENCE, 1776

THE WEALTH OF THE NATION
PAINTING BY SEYMOUR FOGEL

His book was called "An Inquiry into the Nature and Causes of the Wealth of Nations" or "The Wealth of Nations" for short. Smith's book completely changed the way people and governments began to view their economies, so it was a "groundbreaking" book. Eventually, his views had an impact all over the world.

WHAT IS MERCANTILISM?

At the time that Smith was writing, many countries in the world, especially in Europe, had economies that were described as systems of mercantilism. In this system, wealth was an amount that was fixed. To be prosperous, a country had to hold on to precious metals like gold and silver.

SPROTT SILVER BARS

To make even more money, they should sell as much as possible to other countries, but not buy from other countries.

If foreign countries tried to sell to them, they should put tariffs or taxes on those goods so they would be more expensive than their own goods.

In this system, wealth was finite, which simply means that a country couldn't continue to gain more and more wealth. One of the many problems with mercantilism was that countries would add more and more tariffs on goods coming from others. The tariffs got so expensive that it destroyed the chance for trade from country to country. Adam Smith thought this system wasn't wise and he set out to explain theories that he believed would help the economies of countries so they would become more prosperous.

ADAM SMITH, 1723

To demonstrate why tariffs were destructive, he used an example about producing wine in his home country of Scotland. The climate in Scotland isn't good for growing grapes, so hothouses would have to be used to grow them. However, the heating costs would make the wine much too expensive compared to other countries, such as France, where the natural climate was good for wine.

It didn't make any sense for Scotland to produce its own wine and waste money to do it. To make sure that Scottish people would buy the expensive wine made in Scotland, huge tariffs would be charged on the wine that France wanted to sell to them.

WINERY

Smith argued that France had an advantage in the competition for wine due to its climate.

Scotland had an advantage in producing wool, so it would make much more sense for Scotland to import wine from France and export wool.

THE THEMES OF "THE WEALTH OF NATIONS"

Smith had many important themes woven into his book. His ideas were new and different when they were introduced, but today many of his ideas are part of our everyday economy.

ADAM SMITH STATUE IN EDINBURGH

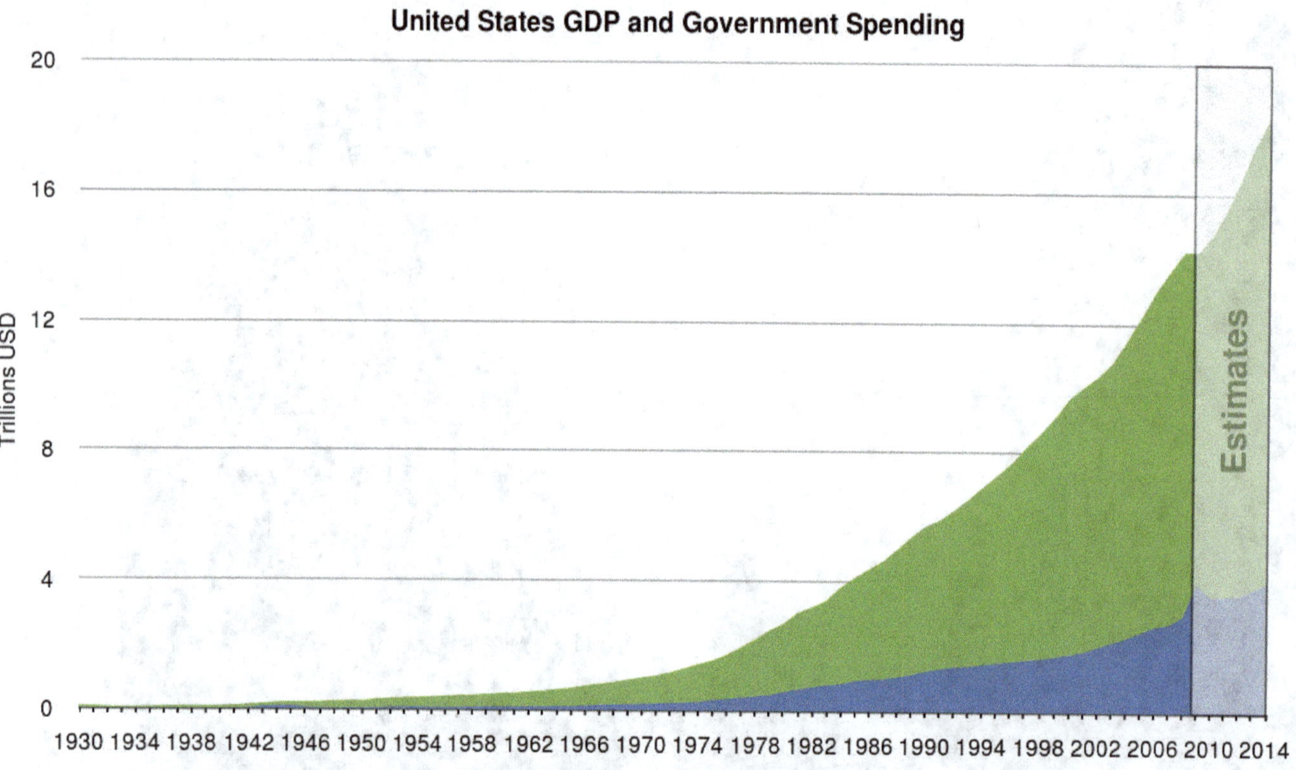

US FEDERAL OUTLAY AND GDP LINEAR GRAPH

THE GOVERNMENT SHOULDN'T REGULATE COMMERCE

Smith didn't believe that a nation's wealth was only in the gold and silver it hoarded. His new insight was that prosperity was actually the free exchange of goods as well as services. This exchange should take place within a country and also from country to country without any government restrictions. Today, we call that wealth our country's "gross national product" or GNP for short.

In order to increase a country's GNP, its capacity to produce had to be as free as possible. Smith felt that the government had many important roles, but regulating the economy wasn't one of them.

The government should protect the nation from attacks by other nations. It should also offer education for all its citizens, so that people can continue to improve themselves.

He also felt that the government should enforce people's rights to property as well as contracts. It was his firm belief that a country's government shouldn't regulate its economy in any artificial way. He realized that the government might need people to pay taxes, however, he felt it was important that taxes be levied based on an individual's ability to send that payment with ease.

Taxes shouldn't be arbitrary or punishing. He also felt that the government shouldn't tax capital excessively since it's important for businesses to re-invest capital to boost productivity.

He felt it was important for governments to be careful with their spending and not build up massive debts.

DIVISION OF LABOR

Smith believed that the way that labor is divided could make it more efficient and therefore more profitable. In other words, if a product needs to be manufactured it can be done more efficiently if the process is broken down into small step-by-step tasks and each task is completed by a specialist. The profit from this "division of labor" would mean that businesses and countries could invest in more machines to save labor too.

ACCUMULATION OF CAPITAL

Smith wrote that a country's potential for future income was dependent on how much capital it could accumulate. The word "capital" here means anything that has value, such as money, property, or precious metals. The more efficient production processes became, and the more capital that was collected, saved, and then invested, the more future prosperity there could be. As capital grows, everyone achieves a better standard of living and becomes more prosperous.

UNITED STATES OF AMERICA
$1

However, the people in the nation must feel that the government has their best interests at heart. They need to feel certain that if they accumulate wealth that it won't be stolen from them.

They don't want the government to squander the nation's wealth. Over time, the countries that will become the most prosperous are those that increase their capital as well as manage it efficiently and protect it.

ENLIGHTENED SELF-INTEREST

Smith believed that most business people are hard working and can be frugal if they understand the benefits of saving and investing. He believed that it was good for people to act in their own self-interest. However, the merchant's self-interest would be changed by what customers desire and would pay for.

STATUE OF ADAM SMITH

oday, we would call this a "win-win" for the merchant and for the consumer. This process of making every transaction workable for both sides is what he meant by "enlightened." He used an example of a butcher to explain this idea. A butcher doesn't supply meat to his customers because he is generous. He does it for one reason only. He wants to make a profit so that he can feed his own family.

Another reason is he wants to accumulate capital so he can invest in a better property or better machines. Then, his business can become even more profitable. If he sells meat that isn't of good quality or if he sells it at too high of a price, he won't gain the customers he needs.

They will go elsewhere to buy their meat. However, if he's able to provide excellent meat at a fair price, he and his customers will both benefit every time they buy from him.

MAGO

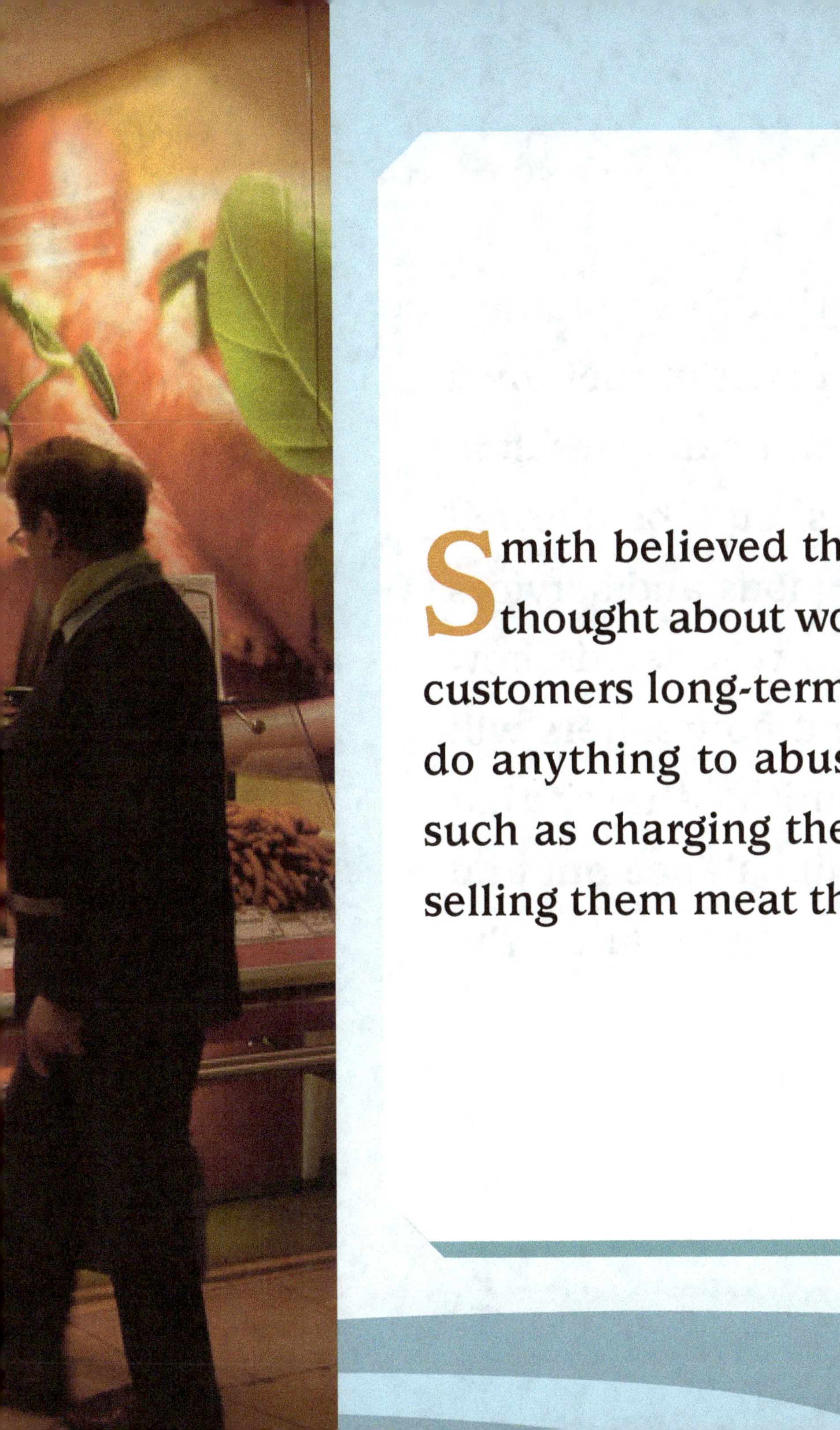

Smith believed that if merchants thought about working with their customers long-term, they wouldn't do anything to abuse their buyers, such as charging them too much or selling them meat that was spoiled.

Smith believed that this tendency for merchants to act in their own self-interest would ultimately result in prosperity. People should be allowed to create and sell goods and services freely. Competition will decide how buyers will buy and how sellers will sell. Ultimately, Smith believed that a free economy will balance out and an "invisible" hand will guide the process.

He didn't mean that someone's hand would actually be there. He just meant that if you look at what a merchant has to offer and it is too expensive for the value they offer, you'll buy it from someone else instead.

If a merchant isn't selling enough goods to be prosperous, he or she will have to lower the price to get more customers.

nother possibility is to offer something that others aren't offering, then he or she can charge more because that product or service is scarce. This process happens automatically with the "invisible hand" in a free market that isn't controlled by artificial government regulations.

Market
Investing activities
Capital expenditures
Purchases of restauran
Financ
Net shor
ong-te
Cash P
Incom
her a
Ac

6549
COMPTOIR LINGOTS - PARIS
999.9
E 3401
E 1768

A CURRENCY BACKED BY PRECIOUS METALS

Smith believed that it was important for a nation to have what is called a "hard currency." A strong nation has a currency that doesn't fluctuate much in value. One of the ways to keep a currency strong is to have precious metals backing up its value.

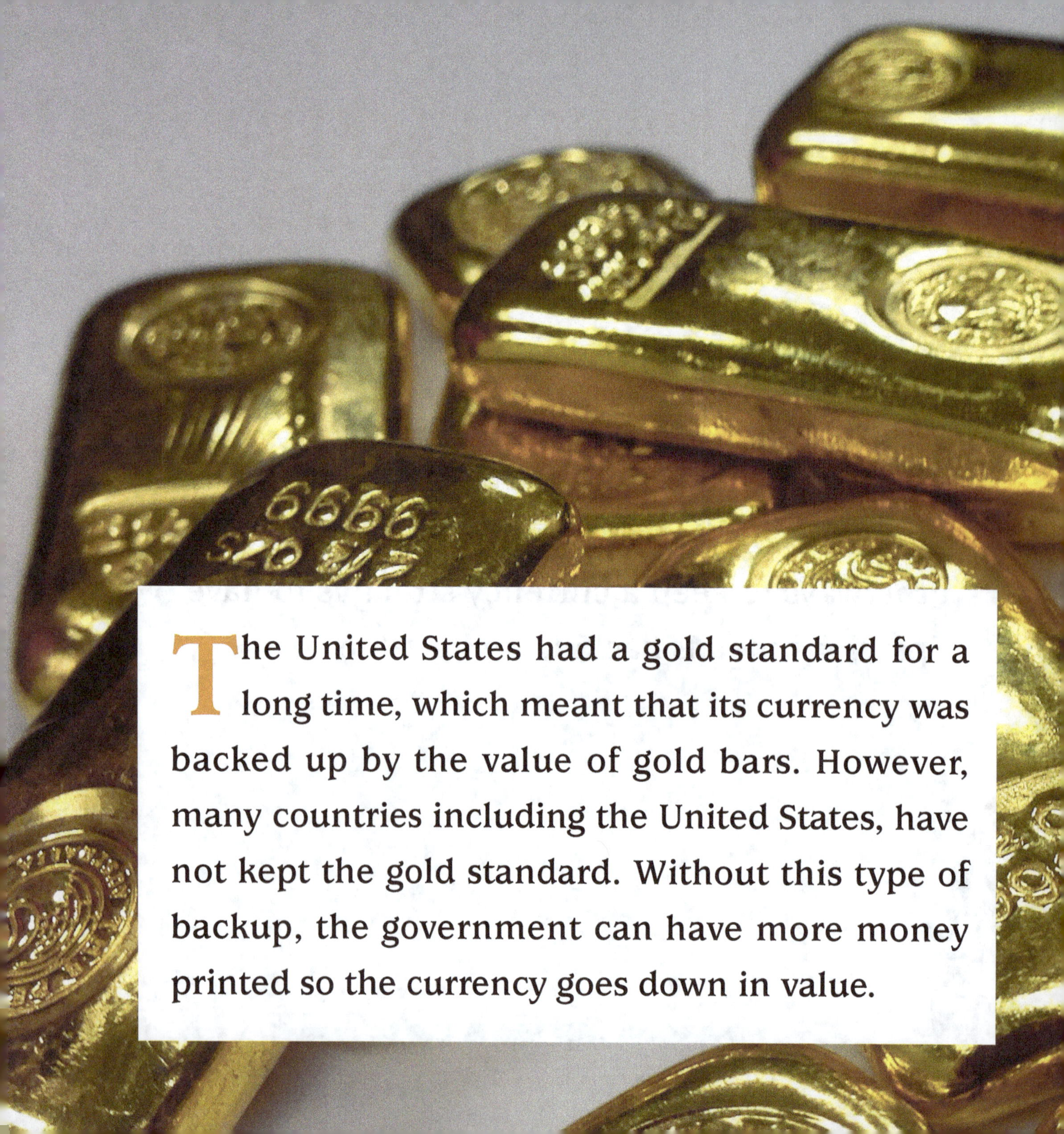

The United States had a gold standard for a long time, which meant that its currency was backed up by the value of gold bars. However, many countries including the United States, have not kept the gold standard. Without this type of backup, the government can have more money printed so the currency goes down in value.

There's also a potential that there will be wasteful spending for unnecessary wars or other expenses. Today, there aren't any countries in the world that back up their money with a gold standard although many, including the United States, have gold stockpiles.

Countries with strong governments and stable political systems usually don't have much fluctuation in the value of their money.

SUMMARY

dam Smith was a Scottish philosopher and economist who wrote an important book called "The Wealth of Nations." He believed that nations should get away from their system of mercantilism and go to a free market economy.

His theories stated that if buyers and sellers had a free market, an "invisible hand" would guide the process so that the economy would reach a profitable balance without government tariffs or interference.

Awesome! Now that you've read about Adam Smith's theories, you may want to read about how to manage your own personal finances in the Baby Professor book A Kid's Guide to Personal Finance – Money Book for Children.

Visit

BABY PROFESSOR
EDUCATION KIDS

www.BabyProfessorBooks.com

to download Free Baby Professor eBooks
and view our catalog of new and exciting
Children's Books

www.ingramcontent.com/pod-product-compliance
Lightning Source LLC
Chambersburg PA
CBHW060221120726

48009CB00003B/99